Cleaning Business

7 Steps To Earing $50,000+ A Year From A Residential Cleaning Business

Introduction

I want to thank you and congratulate you for downloading the book, *"Cleaning Business - 7 Steps To Earing $50,000+ A Year From A Residential Cleaning Business"*.

This book contains proven steps and strategies on how to start a successful cleaning business.

Although it may not seem like it, cleaning is big business. A well step up residential cleaning business can earn you substantial amounts of money (to the tune of $50,000+ per year). However, many people intent on starting this business tend to underestimate the amount of preparation and effort that goes into establishing such a business. After all, we all clean, right? Right, but cleaning another person's home for monetary gains/fee is infinitely different from cleaning your residence. When the word 'business' enters into the picture, a lot changes. Suddenly, the differences become clear: the person you are cleaning for expects value for money.

If you are keen on starting a profitable residential cleaning business that provides value to its clients, you need to avoid common pitfalls made by beginners venturing into this business. Fortunately, this book, has everything you need to create a profitable and immensely valuable cleaning business.

This guide will teach you how to get started on the business. The book will also look at the intricacies of owning and running a successful residential cleaning business. You will learn the pros and cons of this type of business, the items you need to set up the business and get started, how to market your business for maximum exposure once it is up and running, how to price cleaning jobs, how to build a brand that stands out from the competition, and many more.

Thanks again for downloading this book, I hope you enjoy it!

© **Copyright 2016 by** _____ **- All rights reserved.**

This document is geared towards providing exact and reliable information in regards to the topic and issue covered. The publication is sold with the idea that the publisher is not required to render accounting, officially permitted, or otherwise, qualified services. If advice is necessary, legal or professional, a practiced individual in the profession should be ordered.

- From a Declaration of Principles which was accepted and approved equally by a Committee of the American Bar Association and a Committee of Publishers and Associations.

In no way is it legal to reproduce, duplicate, or transmit any part of this document in either electronic means or in printed format. Recording of this publication is strictly prohibited and any storage of this document is not allowed unless with written permission from the publisher. All rights reserved.

The information provided herein is stated to be truthful and consistent, in that any liability, in terms of inattention or otherwise, by any usage or abuse of any policies, processes, or directions contained within is the solitary and utter responsibility of the recipient reader. Under no circumstances will any legal responsibility or blame be held against the publisher for any reparation, damages, or monetary loss due to the information herein, either directly or indirectly.

Respective authors own all copyrights not held by the publisher.

The information herein is offered for informational purposes solely, and is universal as so. The presentation of the information is without contract or any type of guarantee assurance.

The trademarks that are used are without any consent, and the publication of the trademark is without permission or backing by the trademark owner. All trademarks and brands within this book are for clarifying purposes only and are the owned by the owners themselves, not affiliated with this document.

Table of Contents

Cleaning Business

7 Steps To Earing $50,000+ A Year From A Residential Cleaning Business

Introduction

Chapter 1: Getting Started

Chapter 2: The Benefits And Challenges Of A Residential Cleaning Business

Chapter 3: Basic Supplies Needed To Start

Chapter 4: Marketing Your Business - Powerful Marketing Tactics

Chapter 5: Powerful Branding That Beats Your Competition

Chapter 6: How To Price Jobs Right For Maximum Profit

Chapter 7: Keeping Clients Long-Term

Conclusion

Chapter 1: Getting Started

To get started, the first thing you need to do is develop a business mentality. Remember, cleaning for monetary gains is different from cleaning your home; therefore, to make it in this business, you must go about setting up your residential cleaning business professionally.

Here, you need to consider several things such as:

Pick Your Business Name

A business name lets people know you are not engaging in a passing fantasy: you are a business that takes the cleaning seriously. A business name shows potential clients and other businesses your seriousness towards the cleaning business and your intent to treat clients and their homes in a professional manner. So, how exactly do you pick a suitable business name for your company?

How to Pick a Business Name for Your Cleaning Business

When choosing a name, you should exercise caution. You should choose a name that reflects your business values and lets people know what you do. Many business owners in this type of business use their own name followed by 'cleaning service'. A good example is "Big Joe's Cleaning Service".

Once you decide on a suitable name, the next thing you need to do is do a business name search in the business name registry to ensure that you on not infringing on another person's copyright. In some cases, you may potentially use the same name as another business if you are not in the same trade.

A point to note is that when selecting a name, also consider things such as future business expansion, social media presence, and branding potential. Once you consider these things, note down some options, and wait awhile before adopting your business name.

Get A Business License

Your business must be legal and adhere to local laws and regulations. To ensure this legality, you need a business license. You can get more information about getting a license by contacting your county licensing offices. In particular, contact city hall, the county clerk's office, or any department set aside for doing business in the city you live. In most cases, a **DBA** (doing business as) license will be all you shall need. However, some cities may call for an occupational license. A DBA license lets you operate your business using other names. Getting a DBA requires filling a DBA form.

Apart from getting a DBA license, you also need to open a DBA Bank Account. While this is not mandatory, it is advisable, as you don't want cases of mixing your business money with your personal money. However, it is important to note that a DBA bank account will not exempt your personal assets from risk should your business become a liability. Basically, it makes record keeping much easier as well as for tax purposes.

The only thing you need to set up a DBA account is your social security number instead of a separate federal ID.

To avoid later frustration and disappointment, it is vital that you start looking into your DBA as soon as possible. If the name you want to use is unavailable, you will have to come up with another name, something if not taken care of as you get started, may interfere with your branding and social media presence.

Get Business Insurance

When going into business, you MUST seriously think about getting some insurance. When you are in the business of cleaning residential homes, several things can go wrong. You can accidentally break expensive items; you can be injured, etc.

To ensure your protection, you need insurance. You can opt to get general liability insurance, but you should consider other types of insurance such as:

Lost Key Coverage

As you go about residential cleaning, you will have some clients who will ask you to lock up after cleaning. If you lose the keys, you will have to replace the keys or install new locks. This can cost a pretty penny depending on the types of locks. The lost key coverage insurance covers this.

Property Coverage

Sometimes, you need to rent cleaning equipment for specific cleaning jobs. Once you hire, it means you will be responsible for such property until you return them to their respective owners. If while under your care, such property is damaged, you will need to cover the cost of repair or new purchase. The property coverage saves you the hassle and trouble.

Theft of Customer Property Coverage

In the course of doing business, you may forget to lock up after cleaning, an action that may lead to stolen property. In this case, you will be guilty of negligence and you will be required to pay for the lost items. Additionally, you may employ someone who ends up stealing from your clients. This type of insurance insures you against such scenarios, which lessens your financial burden.

Limited Pollution Coverage

Cleaning obviously involves the use of various cleaning agents. Most of these agents contain chemicals that can be dangerous to human beings and animals. In case of accidental job site pollution to your employees, it would be best to have some insurance. This type of insurance covers you against such predicaments.

Business Income Coverage

Small businesses depend on clients for their continued survival. However, as it often happens, clients can stop using your services. This can financially set you back. If you are not careful, you can go out of business altogether.

In instances where your biggest clients stop doing business with you, business income coverage gives you the time needed to look for new clients and turn things around.

Note: When getting insurance coverage for your business, do not deal with any insurance broker. Instead, select a knowledgeable broker who can help you fully understand the insurance that will work best for you.

About Residential Cleaning Business Taxes

As is with any business, when conducting a residential cleaning business (RCB), you will need to pay taxes. For tax purposes, you will need to decide the type of entity you will be filling the business as. You can decide on Limited liability company, Limited liability partnership or sole proprietorship. Choose, what best suits your needs. Once you settle on something, you need to apply for a tax identification number. This informs the IRS that you run a business and they can give you the necessary information on business and employment tax.

If you intend to have employees, you will be required to get a federal tax ID.

Get a business phone number

When you are an entrepreneur, separating your business and personal life is always a good idea. If you fail to segregate these areas of your life, one will intrude into the other very easily.

A good way to separate your business from your personal life is to have a business phone used only for conducting business. When getting a business phone number, consult your phone company for options.

Chapter 2: The Benefits And Challenges Of A Residential Cleaning Business

Even though it has its fair share of anxiety, starting your own business is a thrilling venture. However, like many businesses out there, starting a residential cleaning business has its challenges as well. In this chapter, we will look at how you stand to benefit by starting a residential cleaning business as well as some challenges to look out for so that you are better equipped to handle them.

The Pros

You can set your own limits

When you own a business, you are the boss. As such, you get to determine how far you want to go. This gives you freedom to organize your time and choose jobs that you actually want to do.

Because you are the boss, you will also have the freedom to create your own work environment because you will not have to constantly deal with colleagues. You can decide when to work, when to take breaks, if to work over the weekends and what work to accomplish first before dealing with other things.

You get a good amount of profit

You are in this business because you want to earn some money. Well, a residential cleaning business makes this possible. Unless you come to some sort of agreement with a client, say for instance, a client keeps you on retainer and pays you on a monthly basis; most cleaning jobs have immediate payouts once you complete the job. Instant rewards can keep you motivated and keep your business cash flow steady.

You can expand your business

When you own and run a residential cleaning business, your expansion potential is limitless. Many people who start the business solo soon find themselves having to employ others to keep up with the demand. If you play your cards well, your cleaning business will grow beyond you, and perhaps beyond residential home cleaning to office cleaning, mall cleaning, car detailing, etc.

You get invaluable experience

Starting a business gives you invaluable experience that prepares you for future success. When you own a business, you learn how to manage yourself, manage others, manage finances, and deal with various issues and challenges. This experience reflects in your day-to-day life.

The Challenges

In as much as a residential cleaning business has tons of pros, it is not without its cons. Some of these cons are:

Takes a toll on physical stamina

When you start out, you may have to do the cleaning before you can scale up and employ people. Since, cleaning requires physical strength, if you are unfit, you will quickly tire. You may fall into exhaustion before you realize what is happening. For this reason, you must exercise at least a few times each week. The good thing is that over time, you can employ people to help you and you will not have to do everything on your own.

It can take an emotional toll

Starting and running a business demands a lot from you. You need to know how you are going to finance the business, how to deal with employees, how to manage clients, how to ensure that you offer the best cleaning services among other things. This is all emotionally draining and if you don't know how to manage your time well, you will be one stressed person.

You will have pressure to perform

Cleaning is one of those businesses where you cannot afford to do shoddy work. Whenever your clients use your services, they expect excellent work.

In an effort to ensure you are doing a thorough job, some clients use tactics such as hiding things all over the house to see if you will find them. If your client is unhappy with you cleaning, you will lose that client.

Added Responsibility

The thing about having your own business, it is that your business is primarily your responsibility. You have to ensure that everything is in order. You have to find clients and ensure they get top-notch service. If something goes wrong, you will have to deal with it and answer any questions the client may have. Even if you employ others, ultimately, you are responsible for them. This added responsibility can take a toll on you.

Before starting a residential cleaning business, reflect on these pros and cons so you can understand what you are getting yourself into. This will help you physically and mentally prepare for the responsibility of being a business owner. When you are adequately prepared, you increase your chances of success.

Chapter 3: Basic Supplies Needed To Start

Just because you are cleaning someone's house does not mean the person should provide the required tools. To achieve success and leave a lasting impression on your clients, be fully prepared. Full preparation will ensure you tackle a job to a client's satisfaction.

Although this preparation has many strings to its bow, one way to prepare is by ensuring you have all necessary supplies. Supplies you need include:

Trash Picking Tools

When you are cleaning residential homes, picking up trash is inevitable. Thus, you must prepare for it. For this purpose, you can use trash bags. However, when dealing with anything you consider trash, be careful. Handle everything with care and place it in a bin where the homeowner can sort through it for anything of importance.

Caddy

As you clean, you will need somewhere to keep all your tools and supplies. A caddy serves this purpose very well. You can place your brushes, toilet cleaners, cleaning cloths and spray bottles in the caddy. This will make it easier to move your tools from place to place.

Brooms

A house broom is multi-purpose and can clean well, but if you will be dealing with large surfaces, consider investing in a push broom. You will also need a dustpan.

Vacuums

When you want to get rid of dust in carpets and in couches, a vacuum cleaner will be your go to tool. You can use various [types of vacuum cleaners](). Ensure the one you select is suitable for the work at hand. Familiarize yourself with the functionalities of your preferred vacuum so you can efficiently use it.

Toilet Cleaning Tools

When cleaning bathrooms, you need various tools. You will need a bowl cleaner to clean the surfaces depending on the condition of the surface you are cleaning. You will also do well to have a stainless steel cleaner for surfaces such as sinks and grab bars that need that extra shine.

You will also need a bowl brush and grout brush to clean the bowl and surfaces with grout lines. Lastly, you will need cleaning clothes. You should have different cloths for things such as sinks, counters, toilets, and mirrors. A good trick is to color code the cloths so you do not forget which ones to use for which location.

You will need various spray bottles for disinfectants and cleaners. Appropriately label each spray bottle to avoid mixing their use.

Wringer and Mop

Mopping forms a huge part of residential cleaning. You need to mop the floor and various surfaces. The obvious tools you need are a mop bucket or wringer and the mop itself (mop handle and head). To avoid damage and the expense of buying a new one, handle mops with care. After using them, clean and dry them well.

Dusting Tools

Sometimes, before you go about cleaning, you will need to dust. For this, you will need things such as duster, furniture polish, microfiber clothes, and an extension duster that allows you access to all you cannot reach without using a ladder.

Protective Clothing

You need to set aside clothes you will wear when you are cleaning. These clothes should be comfortable and allow you to move in various directions. You also need to acquire gloves, aprons, and face masks. When you clean dusty surfaces, you will also need something to cover your head to minimize the amount of dirt getting to your head.

Most of the above items are readily available at the household section of your local supermarket. However, before you decide which items to buy (you need most of these essentials), Shop around because prices for these items vary from shop to shop.

Determine what you need and how much you want to spend. Renting some things like carpet cleaning equipment may seem like a good idea, but if you intend to clean carpets regularly, you should look into purchasing such equipment.

Once you have everything you need to get started, you are ready to go out there and start cleaning. However, before you can bank some cleaning money, your newly created business needs some clients. This calls for a vigorous marketing campaign, which is what we shall look at in chapter 4.

Chapter 4: Marketing Your Business - Powerful Marketing Tactics

Marketing propels your business growth. It also lets potential clients know that you exist, that you provide certain services, and that they can indeed use your services. Although there are various ways to market your residential cleaning business, for a completely new business, the best form of marketing is word of mouth, below are the most effective marketing strategies.

Business Cards

Business cards tell people who you are, what you do, as well as how they can get in touch with you. Many companies provide business card services at a small fee. If you are design adept, you can also design your own cards and print them on your home printer or the local library. Effective business cards are simple and compelling. Create simple and compelling business cards that reflect professionalism. Ensure that the font used is legible and that the card conveys the information that compels action, which in this case is hiring your services.

As you create your business cards, pay attention to your logo and the message it sends. Ensure your logo is clean, precise, and easily identifiable. For branding purposes, also pay attention to the colors you use.

Once your business cards are ready, you can do door-to-door marketing, or set up a booth at a local market/mall/junction and hand them out.

Flyers

Flyers can announce to the neighborhood that a new business is in town. When creating flyers, the thing to remember is that simple and legible works best. Avoid fonts that look nice but are difficult to read from a distance. Ensure your flyers have information detailing what you do and the types of service you offer, and how prospective clients can reach and hire you. Once you have flyers, you can hand them out in different places around the neighborhood. You can also put them up in different places. Ensure that as you do this, you do not break the law.

Door Hangers

To market your business, you can use door hangers that tell prospects the services you offer. When using these, do not be too obvious, aim to capture attention. The best way to use these is once you identify a specific residential area you would like to prospect, hand them on the handles of the main door.

However, as you do this, wear branded wear with your company name and colors to avoid cases of mistaken identity (some people are very squeamish about people walking up to their doors).

Door-To-Door Sales

Sometimes, marketing your business calls for 'taking the bull by the horns' aka engage in door to door sales. In the quest to find clients for your RCB, you can also use cold calling and even letter writing. Create a plan detailing how you will go about door-to-door sales and start reaching out to people. Keep in mind that you will receive many rejections; that is part of the business. What matters the most is the ones who say yes.

Content Marketing

Many businesses have static websites that show what they do. However, a good way to get clients is by offering free information on issues related to cleaning. For instance, once you get a few clients and start working for them, only to discover that carpet stains are problematic for most of these homeowners, you can create a helpful article detailing how to remove carpet stains.

This type of website content attracts visitors and allows Google to rank your page, which makes it easier for others looking for related cleaning services to find you.

Content marketing very much depends on your ability to write compelling content. Shoddy content will not get you clients. Potential clients need to see you know what you are doing. This way, they will trust you can deliver clean homes.

A good way to perform content marketing is to optimize your content and website for local search. Here is how to optimize your website and content for local search.

Video Marketing/You Tube Channel

Nowadays, businesses thrive on the ability to connect with clients. A great way to connect with customers is through video. In fact, studies agree that people who see videos highlighting your products and services are more likely to use your services than people who do not.

A great way to build exposure for your business is by creating self-help videos. For instance, if most of your clients are having dog-poo stain problems on their carpets, it means dog poo stains on carpet is a rampant problem. You can create a titled how to remove dog poo stains on carpet and show people how to do this. At the end of the video (or below the video on YouTube), you can direct people to your services landing page.

Rewards for Referrals

An effective tactic bound to get you tons of new clients is rewarding your current clients whenever they refer a new client. Start by letting your clients know that you are available for further work. Otherwise, they will assume you already have enough clients. When you let them know of your availability, they will recommend you to others. When they do so, offer a bonus or free service. This way, you will encourage them to keep recommending you to others.

Chapter 5: Powerful Branding That Beats Your Competition

As a startup, you must strive to build a brand. A brand differentiates you from your competition and gives you certain advantages over your competition. Let us look at how you benefit by creating a professional brand.

Importance Of Creating A Professional Brand

Apart from differentiating you from your competitors, branding also:

Improves Recognition

For a minute, think of major brands in the business world. When you see their names, you do not doubt what they are selling and how successful they are. You recognize them because they took time to create a brand. Branding improves recognition. Although your branding may be small scale, for example, recognition as the cleaner who effectively cleans dog poo out of carpet, you must start building your brand.

Creates Trust

Branding creates trust simply because it takes effort to build a successful brand. When you create a brand, people will know that they can trust your business because they have heard good things about your brand.

Spearheads Advertising

Advertising is all about letting people know about your business. However, if you are unsure of how to proceed, advertising becomes difficult. To advertise your business extensively, you need to know your vision, mission, and objectives. As you define your brand, you get to know these things.

Creates a Sense of Family

Branding is not just for the benefit of clients. It also works well to develop a sense of family for employees. Your clients feel valued when they receive special treatment. When you invite your clients in and ensure that your employees know what the company is about, everyone will be on the same page, which will ensure your clients get the best services and this means you have loyal customers.

How to Create a Brand for Your RCB

There are several ways to brand your business. Some of these include:

Create a Professional Website

A good way to establish yourself as a professional is to create a business website. You should have a services page that lets visitors know all the services you have to offer. You should also have a landing page that introduces your business to potential clients. This page should include your business name, owner's name, phone numbers, fax number, and address. It is advisable to have several testimonials from clients who have already used your services.

Social Media Page

Social media is a good way to build your brand because it allows you to highlight your business and connect with clients. Before jumping onto the social media wagon, determine which social media forum you are comfortable with (and the one most prospective clients use) and learn everything you can about that forum.

Next, create your posts and posting schedule. Potential clients will be interested to see photos and videos of your work environment. Other social media platforms such as Facebook also allow you to create ads targeting specific demographics and localities. You can use this to your advantage.

Further, create compelling posts that drive engagement and ensure once the engagement starts trickling in, you remain engaged and answer customer's queries.

Have Professional Uniforms

Do not underestimate the importance of uniforms to a business such as a cleaning one. Uniforms present a professional image that your clients will learn to associate with your business. It tells employees that they are a team, and it serves as advertisement for your business because people who see you can inquire about your services.

However, your uniforms should not impede the cleaning job. They should be comfortable and professional looking.

Have a Professional Logo

A professional logo should be part of your branding plan. An effective logo should have your business name, your motto, and an image that best reflects your business. You can use sites like Fiverr to get someone to create your professional logo.

Use Car Billboard

You can put your car to good use by turning it into a moving billboard. Your business name and phone number should be prominent so that people can quickly see it even if your car is moving. You can also have car magnets to advertise.

Chapter 6: How To Price Jobs Right For Maximum Profit

You are in the residential cleaning business to earn a living. This means for maximum profit, you have to price your services right. When pricing your services, there are three things you can consider - the number of rooms that need cleaning, the square footage of the house, and the hours spent cleaning.

Determine which works best for you. Another important thing you should consider is the type of cleaning. There are:

Typical Regular Cleaning

Regular cleaning rates are $25 -$45 per hour. Regular cleaning usually excludes things such as carpet cleaning and wall cleaning. In the cleaning business, the profit you make should be between 10 - 28 percent of your gross sales. You can also search online and find out the pricing or different cleaning services. This way, you will be in a better position to determine how much you should charge to become profitable.

Additional Costs

You can offer other cleaning services such as carpet cleaning, window cleaning, wall cleaning, oven cleaning, and fridge cleaning. Additional costs such as fridge cleaning usually go for $25. However, you need to consider the effort, materials, and any special treatment a service will require before deciding on the price.

Discounted Costs

When your clients are loyal, offer them discounted packages to encourage repeat clients. Take this opportunity to let them know of other services you offer.

Avoid falling into the trap of charging too low or charging too high. To determine your rates, check around to see what other people are charging. Always remember that you are offering valuable service and that you deserved adequate compensation for your hard work.

Chapter 7: Keeping Clients Long-Term

Now that you have a running business, your next goal is to keep clients for the long term. How can you achieve this?

Have Top-Notch Customer Service

Many businesses dedicate a whole department to customer service and for good reason. These businesses are well aware of the impact customer service has on their business. Customer service is important for various reasons including:

It makes your clients feel valued

The way you treat your clients will show them your level of care or lack thereof. Paying clients want to feel valued. After all, they are parting with their money. When your clients feel valued, they begin to feel comfortable doing business with you. So, how can you make your clients feel valued? For starters, always listen to your clients, answer their questions in a timely manner, and solve any issues that may arise; above all, do your work well, and treat your clients with respect.

It reflects on your business

We make judgments depending on what we see and hear. If you treat someone badly, he or she will conclude you will do the same to his or her house. Yes, how you deal with customers' associates with how you conduct your business. If you are a professional, clients will come to you because they know you will provide professional services in other areas.

It is a marketing strategy

Long-term clients make life easier because when you have them, you do not have to worry about finding new clients. Long-term clients also tell others about your business. Thus, if you are wise, you will learn how to treat your clients with the utmost care.

It only takes a few minutes to think of how you want to treat your clients. It costs nothing to show your clients you care and that you value your relationship with them. This will come out in how you speak to them and how you address their issues. Great customer service will help you keep clients.

Provide High Quality Work

After everything, your clients expect you to provide high quality work. It is why they are paying you and it is only fitting that you deliver the best work possible. To do this, you should:

Listen to your clients

It is good to remember that your client is paying for your service because he or she believes you can meet his or her needs. Thus, it is reasonable to listen to what those needs are so you can know how best to fulfill them. Some clients may have certain demands or lists of things they expect you to do. Take it upon yourself to see how best to deliver.

Know your job

Where the cleaning business is concerned, you cannot afford to be ignorant. Listening to your clients does not mean foregoing everything you know about the cleaning business. Never forget that you are the expert. Your client may have heard about a certain product or a certain cleaning method and may ask you to use that.

It is up to you to gauge the situation and advice your client accordingly. This means that you need to be an expert at what you do. Learn about as many cleaning products as you can and how to clean various surfaces and items.

Go the extra mile

Do not be satisfied with providing the bare minimum service to your clients, go the extra mile. There are things you can do that will show your clients that you really care about them and that you know what you are doing.

For example, when cleaning a home, ensure that you do not break anything, trample on flowers, or damage property. Take care of your client's property as if it were your own. You should also never be complacent because you have become familiar with your client or because you have been in the cleaning business for a long time. You can avoid this by having a checklist and ensuring you always maintain high cleaning standards. This will help you maintain long-term clients.

Always Be Honest

Where business is concerned, honesty is a highly valued trait especially when you are dealing with individual clients who have to invite you into their personal homes. When you are honest, your client knows they can rely on you and they are happy to do so. To become an honest businessperson, you need to:

Keep your promises

One way to maintain honesty is to strive to keep your promises. You should avoid promising things you know you cannot deliver. You should also avoid setting deadlines you cannot achieve. Be aware of your limits and your strengths. This way, when you promise your client something, you will keep your promise.

Fix your mistakes

Because you are human, the concept of making mistakes is not foreign to you. However, when it comes to business, mistakes can be costly especially if you try to cover them up. In the course of cleaning, you may end up damaging something or may do something the client feels is not right or well done. Instead of becoming defensive, own your mistake and figure out ways to fix it.

It is important to understand that your clients value honesty and so should you. Do not try to cheat your clients or make them believe that something is good when you know another thing can do the same work at cheaper rates. It would be best to give your clients the information they need to make the final decision. When you provide honest value and feedback, your clients will reciprocate by using your services for the long-term.

Conclusion

Thank you again for downloading this book!

It is important to remember that when you go into the cleaning service business, people are hiring you not because they cannot do the job themselves, but because they do not have to. Your goal should be to provide high quality work that will keep your clients coming back.

When providing residential cleaning services, you should be especially careful to find the right balance between professionalism and friendliness. You will be entering many people's personal space. Your clients need to trust that you will treat their home with respect and continue to provide the best service possible. Remaining professional will ensure you provide quality service to your return clients and that you keeping earning from a residential cleaning business.

Finally, if you enjoyed this book, would you be kind enough to leave a review for this book on Amazon?

Click here to leave a review for this book on Amazon!

Thank you and good luck!

www.ingramcontent.com/pod-product-compliance
Lightning Source LLC
Chambersburg PA
CBHW021449170526
45164CB00001B/449